LESSONS FROM MY FATHERS

*A Tribute to the Men
Who Helped Me Become a Man*

Karl Bernard

DEDICATION

To my Dad

No words could adequately describe the impact you've made on my life. You are still the kindest and most patient man that I have ever met. You took care of me when I couldn't take care of myself. Thank you for giving me the opportunity to return the favor! No matter what I've accomplished or will accomplish, the privilege of being your "father" was and remains one of the greatest periods in my life! Until we meet again….RIH!

To my Children

To Julian, my firstborn. Thank you for being an incredible son and for enduring the "parental trial and error" that comes with being first! I am constantly amazed by your temperament and your ability to see the best in everyone! Clearly, you are the leader the world is waiting for.

To Jonathan, my baby-boy! Your uncanny ability to comprehend what truly matters is astounding. Your personality is magnetic and your ability to accomplish anything you set your heart on has been on "display" since day one! Your time is now! PS. Patiently, waiting for you and your lovely bride to change my name to Papa! Just saying!

To Kaelie, my daughter. Before you were born, everyone knew there was a missing piece to our family puzzle. Since your arrival, whenever doubt creeps into my heart and mind about God's love for me, immediately, when I look at you, all doubt disappears. Your wisdom and ability to build on lessons learned will change your community and even the world.

I wrote this book to remind each of you that we are standing on someone's shoulders. So always, always be grateful, humble and kind!

Table of Contents

Forward

By Anthony "Booger" McFarland

Former LSU Tiger, First Team All American, 1999 NFL 1ˢᵗ Round Draft Selection, two-time Superbowl Champion, sports commentator and pregame analyst on ESPN's Monday Night Countdown

I have been blessed with the opportunity to meet and get to know many great and wonderful people. However, no person has impacted my life any more than Karl Bernard ("KB"). He has been my agent, lawyer, confidant, counselor and a good friend to me and my family. My entire family loves KB. What I describe below, typifies our relationship.

Not long after I signed my first NFL contract (in which KB was able to bypass the "slotting" mechanism), KB and I had a conversation about my future after football. I tried to terminate the conversation immediately. He didn't take the hint. KB insisted that I could be successful at providing commentary and analysis on sporting events after I retired from football. I didn't want to hear what he had to say. I told him that he was "doing way too much." All I wanted to do was to become an impact player in the NFL and play in the Super Bowl. I told him that I wasn't interested. But if you know anything about KB, it is hard for him to accept "no" as an answer![1] Because he hadn't brought up the "commentator" conversation for a while, I assumed the issue was dead. But it wasn't. A few years later, he initiated the "commentator" conversation again. This time, he presented me with an opportunity to appear on the sports talk/variety show called "The Best Damn Sports Show Period." Well, as "they" say, "the rest is history." KB has been and continues to be a "father" (and a brother) to me.

Lessons From My Fathers provides an intimate look into how a man has been put together piece by piece. It's often said that it takes a village to raise a child, and this is true. I would also add that it takes men to pour into and cultivate a man. What a great way to understand the make-up of one of the sincerest men I know. This book is both motivational and intriguing and, I might add, filled with many "lessons" that can benefit us all as we continue the never-ending journey "to become what we are capable of becoming."

Booger

---

[1] After reading "Lessons from My Fathers," now I know why!

INTRODUCTION

Like many of my childhood friends, I spent a lot of time dreaming about who or what I would become as an adult. I even dreamt about becoming a superhero. Though my superhero dream has not come to pass (yet), many others have. I'm a dad, and I have a few good friends. I'm also a petroleum engineer, an attorney and an adjunct professor of law. I've taught at Tulane University, Loyola School of Law, and LSU's Paul M. Hebert Law Center for a total of 20 years, and I've practiced law for nearly 30 years. Additionally, I've had the opportunity to play in the NFL, and I sang on national television at the 1989 Super Bowl. I've been awarded numerous leadership, athletic and academic awards in law school, college and high school. I married my high school sweetheart and was blessed with three wonderful children, two sons and one daughter, whom I'm extremely proud of. I became a deacon and Chairman of the Deacon Board at the church I attended. I grew up with both parents in the home, in a neighborhood where everybody knew everybody and attended a church where everybody loved everybody.

However, like most individuals over the age of 55, I've gone through many situations that I would not wish on an enemy. My career as a professional athlete ended almost as quickly as it began due to a catastrophic knee injury. When my daughter was just three years old, her pediatrician called and told me that he didn't think she was going to make it. Two of the most important women in my life were diagnosed with cancer. I was the primary caregiver for my dad and mom as they suffered with dementia and Alzheimer's disease. My brother died, and to this day nobody knows how or why. I was responsible for burying my entire "nuclear" family, and my high school sweetheart and I are divorced. And that's not all. While the divorce was pending, I had to resign my position as Chairman of the Deacon Board and several of my "closest" friends ended all communication with me. I can honestly say that every success I've experienced and every victory I've enjoyed has been tempered by circumstances that have tempted me to give up, give in or give out.[2] However, I am proud to report that although I have, on occasion, given up, I have never given in or given out. I'M STILL STANDING!!!

I'm still standing because the good Lord has always placed one or more "fathers" in my life to protect me, direct me, encourage me and correct me! Some of my fathers are black and some are white. Some are older than I am and some are younger. Some are military veterans and some are pastors. Some I knew very well and some I only knew from afar. Because life can be painfully hard, without my fathers, I most assuredly would have given in or given out. Thus, I am a living witness that God works in and through people. Put simply, I'm fully persuaded that the answers to most, if not all, of life's dilemmas can be found in the love and unity that can only be realized when people make the time to form, fix and foster relationships with one another.[3] Because several men took the time to enter into relationship with me, I wrote this book to celebrate the many contributions that they've made to my life, and by proxy, to the lives of the people I've formed relationships with.

---

[2] Though many may consider *giving up*, *giving in*, and *giving out* to be synonymous, for me to *give up* means to get out of a situation or circumstance or to change direction, location or personnel; to *give in* means to remain in a situation or circumstance and to allow it to change you or your desires, purpose or values; and to *give out* means to stop pursing the purpose for which you believe you were created.

[3] My story would not be complete without a tribute to the "mothers" and the "brothers" in my life. Stay tuned!

My Dad

Alfred Bernard

Background

I grew up in a two-parent home with one sibling, an older brother named Andre. My parents, Alfred and Gloria Bernard, had both obtained master's degrees in their chosen fields of study. My dad was a high school band director, and my mom was a high school English and Free Enterprise instructor. My dad always had a second job, either selling insurance or working at a lumber yard. My mom, on the other hand, would become a fulltime housewife when the school year ended and summer began. She made sure that my brother and I were enrolled in summer camp every summer. My parents were from the old school, which meant my brother and I could not simply do what we felt like doing. For instance, we could not give our parents a one-word answer to any question or request. No matter how we felt, every response had to end with "sir" or "ma'am."

My parents had very specific roles in the family. My mom was responsible for cooking and doing laundry, and my dad was responsible for maintaining the yard and the cars. We all pitched in to keep the house clean and orderly. I don't remember my dad ever missing a day of work, and I only remember my mom missing work when she had her wisdom teeth removed. If they ever argued, it was behind closed doors. Both of my parents believed in God, education, hard work and laughter. My dad knew how to make my mom laugh, and my mom knew how to get my dad to do whatever she wanted him to do. They loved each other immensely. They were married for 53 years until death separated them. However, besides holding hands and an occasional hug or kiss, my parents didn't display a lot of affection in public, or even in front of my brother and me. Again, they were old school. Nevertheless, my brother and I could hear noises from my parents' bedroom when we placed our ears next to the air conditioning vent in our room. That's how we knew our parents really loved each other!

Everybody Is Somebody

My mom was a great cook, and she had an opinion about everybody she met. Relatives and friends would routinely stop by our home to eat my mom's cooking (especially her desserts) and to get a laugh while listening to her opinions about a particular person. Naturally, people either loved my mom or avoided her. My dad, on the other hand, never met a stranger. This was the case even though my dad grew up in a segregated environment. Everybody loved him: strangers, friends, family, his students – both black and white. Nobody left my dad's presence without a smile on their face or without feeling more confident about the future. He remembered the name of every person he met. To accomplish this feat, my dad always carried a 3x5 index card and a pen in his shirt or coat pocket to write down people's names. He believed that a person's name was the sweetest sound to that person's ear. To my dad, "everybody [was] somebody."[4]

Discipline, Honesty and Fun

My dad did not believe in doing anything over again, so he did not take shortcuts. He did everything by the book. It didn't matter if he was

---

[4] My dad adopted this attitude while in college at Grambling State University. He would always talk about GSU President, the late great R.W.E. Jones, who established GSU's motto: "the place where everybody is somebody."

4

changing out a starter on a car or assembling a toy, my dad always followed the manufacturer's written directions. My dad was also incredibly honest. He did not lie, nor did he tolerate lying. He would repeatedly tell my brother and me, "Whatever you do, don't ever lie to me." He believed that honesty was the foundation of any true and lasting relationship with family, friends or colleagues. In fact, the only time I really got in trouble with my dad was when I wasn't being completely truthful with him. As long as I was honest, he readily helped me work through any difficulty.

There was always a get-up time, a curfew and a check-in time in the Bernard household, even on the weekends. My dad would announce to us our wake-up time the night before. With the exception of certain holidays, he didn't believe that his sons should sleep late or just lay in bed. Nevertheless, my brother and I routinely had problems getting out of bed on the weekends. To help us out, my mom would first try to wake us with the smell of bacon and biscuits. That usually did the trick. If not, she would softly call our names. And if that didn't work, the sound of the garage door opening and closing always got my brother and me out of bed and into the bathroom to get cleaned up. That sound was usually my dad coming inside looking for us, or my mom pulling a prank!

During the week, our curfew was determined by the streetlights. When they came on, we had ten minutes to make it home or my mom would come looking for us, which, needless to say, was embarrassing. But she didn't care. In fact, I truly believe my mom enjoyed yelling out of the car window when she pulled up on me with my friends. She would say the same thing every time: "Gregory Bernard! If you don't get your narrow behind home this instant, I will get out of this car and spank your butt in front of your friends!" My friends were my mom's biggest fans. They imitated her all the time!

On the weekend, we had to be in by 10:00pm. When I started driving, I could come in a little later, but I had to call and check in every hour after 10:00pm.[5] At first, I found this very difficult to do when I was out with the "fellas." But I soon wised up. I started having house parties and gatherings at my house instead of going out. But no matter how late I

---

[5] My safety was one of my dad's primary concerns. When I went out with friends, he did not go to bed until I came home and only after a brief conversation (to make sure I was ok).

stayed up on Saturday night, my dad made sure my brother and I were up on Sunday morning to attend church on time.

If any house rule was broken, there were consequences. For the first infraction, my dad would sit us down and make sure we understood the rule and why it was implemented. For the second infraction, we would have to wake up early on the weekend and pull unwanted grass, usually Bermuda grass, from the flower beds and planters for hours. There was no third infraction. Interestingly, I don't recall ever being spanked by my dad. He didn't need to. He and my mom had a "look" that would make me stop whatever I was doing, immediately.

Every Sunday morning, my dad would wash the cars and my mom would prepare Sunday dinner. If it was football season, my dad would turn the TV on and turn the volume up loud so, while washing the cars, he could hear the Grambling State University Fight Song played at the beginning of the GSU Football Show, featuring legendary Coach Eddie Robinson. My dad graduated from Grambling and, while an undergrad, was a member of the GSU marching band.[6]

Like clockwork, my dad would finish washing one of the cars by 9:00am, my brother and I would jump into the car by 9:05, and at 9:10 my mom would drive us to Shiloh Missionary Baptist Church and drop my brother and me off for Sunday school. We were always greeted at the door by the director of Shiloh's Sunday school department, Sister Estell Beauchamp, and our Sunday school teachers, Sister White and Sister Williams. After dropping us off, my mom would rush back home and get ready for the worship service. She was an usher and my dad was a deacon. And my brother and I were good boys – that is, until our friends Dewey Minor and John "Huggy Bear" Holmes arrived at church!

Thanks to extracurricular activities at school, youth activities at church and summer camps, my brother and I were always busy after school and during the summer months. But no matter what and no matter where, my parents were always "there." There to take us to and from practice or a

---

[6] Worth noting, my mom graduated from Southern University in Baton Rouge. My parents supported both Southern and Grambling until the two schools played against each other in football or basketball. Every year they would try to bribe my brother and me to cheer for their school at games. Each year, my brother and I would raise the price for our support.

track meet or game. There to watch us perform. There to encourage us after a bad performance, and there to keep our feet on the ground after a good performance. When I played football or basketball or ran track, I could count on one hand the number of times that I looked into the stands and didn't see at least one of my parents. My dad believed in reminding me, in his own way, that I was "not in this world by myself." Because of my dad, my home was stable, predictable and, most of the time, enjoyable.

Importantly, my dad believed that every relationship should be filled with laughter. He loved to laugh, and he loved to see me, my mom and my brother laugh. He would tickle us – all the time. Once or twice a week my dad would share a funny story or joke with us. He loved sitcoms, especially the Flip Wilson Show and Sanford and Son, and he loved to have fun. To that end, my dad also loved to chase me around the house, inside and out. He would fall out laughing when I "juked" him to avoid contact. He later told me that he was preparing me to play football. I was just having fun. Additionally, my dad always encouraged me to dance and sing for the family. He was my first voice coach and choreographer. Now that I think about it, just about everything I do now I learned, directly or indirectly, from my dad – even how to fish.

Speaking of fishing, it was my dad's one bona fide hobby. He loved to fish. His favorite place to fish was Bayou Pigeon and its surrounding bayous and lakes. We fished that area so much that I could literally find our fishing spots at night with my eyes closed. Some of the greatest experiences in my life occurred on a 19-foot bass boat in Bayou Pigeon with my dad. My dad truly loved life. He taught me that too.

Have a Plan

As noted above, my dad was a high school band director. He taught music for 20 years. The bands he directed routinely marched in parades and competed in corps competitions in and around Louisiana and regularly received invitations to participate in the Disney parade at Disney World in Orlando. Though the parades, competitions and the trips to Florida tested my dad's ability to plan, maintain order and keep everybody smiling, he loved it. Nevertheless, after he completed his twentieth year of teaching, my dad retired. Although his students and their parents cried when he announced his retirement, my dad had a plan. For years, he had been spending time over the summer months learning how to sell insurance. This is because my dad always wanted more than one source of income. After retiring from teaching, he became a fulltime insurance agent, which gave him a second income stream in addition to his retirement income.

My dad began working for New York Life Insurance Co., and unsurprisingly, he hit the ground running. Soon he was regularly earning multiple club awards and roundtable awards. However, because he wanted to be in a position to offer more competitive products and premium payment plans for more of his customers, my dad started his own insurance business. His desire to be of service to others was far stronger than his fear of starting a small business on his own. My dad named his business Bernard and Associates, LLC: Your One Stop Insurance Agency. With his own business, my dad could broker insurance products to his customers from several insurance companies instead of just one. Though my dad's business ended when he died, by any other measure, it was a massive success.

If You're Wrong, Change

To be completely honest, however, my dad was not a perfect man. For most of my childhood, he smoked at least two packs of cigarettes a day. In fact, a low-level cloud of smoke could regularly be seen in the family room, where my dad watched TV most evenings. My dad also drank alcohol two or three times a week. When he drank, instead of becoming more jovial, my dad would become quiet, distant, and start strange conversations with whoever happened to be around. Whenever my brother and I saw my dad drinking, we would immediately leave the family room and go to another part of the house, usually our bedroom. My mom, on the other hand, either found something to do in the kitchen or got on the phone and called one of her good friends. Almost like clockwork, when my dad drank he would have the family room to himself. Me and my brother would then listen through the air vent for noises, any noise. When we would finally hear our dad snoring, then and only then, could we go to bed and get some sleep.

Sometime during my freshman year of high school, the message about smoking and the harmful effects of secondhand smoke finally hit home with my dad. Around the same time, my dad asked me to explain why I would always leave the family room when he drank. I was a bit hesitant, but I told him the truth. I told him that when he drank, he didn't act like my dad anymore, that he was a different person. Not many days later, he stopped smoking and drinking cold turkey. I couldn't believe it! But it was true. My dad quit smoking and drinking at the same time, more or less overnight. He was living proof of what he'd repeatedly drilled into me, that anybody can accomplish anything with a made-up mind.[7]

My dad could change direction faster than anyone I knew. Once he became convinced that the change was positive, he would do it without delay. As illustrated above, my dad was disciplined, consistent and honest. As a result, I grew up in a home that was stable, secure, supportive and predictable. He showed me that you can't have true freedom without discipline and you can't achieve lasting success without being consistent and honest. Moreover, my dad showed me that life was not meant to be lived alone. He loved people, and he loved to see people smile and laugh. He truly believed that a good laugh was medicine to the soul. Not surprisingly, I've tried to emulate my father in just about every aspect of my life. Not a day goes by that I don't thank God for my dad. My dad was and still is my superhero! He gave me a name that I'm proud to call my own and to pass on to my children and he told me how to best learn and appreciate life in America – own and operate a business. He was right. Thanks dad!

---

[7] My dad died on April 19, 2012 – about eight months after learning of my brother's death and three weeks after my mom no longer remembered who he was, her Alzheimer's having progressed to that awful state. Although my dad's doctors gave several medical explanations for his death, because I knew my dad, I knew the real cause of his death was a broken heart.

VILLAGE FATHERS

Neighborhood Fathers

I grew up in a nearly all-black environment. I was born at Flint Goodrich Hospital in New Orleans, a hospital for black people and administered by black people. I grew up in all-black neighborhoods in Baton Rouge: Easy Town and Scotlandville. In Easy Town, I learned how to ride a bike, make mud pies, protect myself from bullies, swim on a rain- flooded street and what it meant to be a high school girl's "lil" boyfriend. I also learned how important it was to have "good" neighbors – people who maintained their property and desired to live peaceably. Growing up, my family was surrounded by good neighbors next door and across the street. We could count on them and they could count on us – for anything!

From elementary school through high school, I lived in Park Vista, or PV, a subdivision located in Scotlandville. PV was unique because it was only a five-minute drive or a 20-minute walk from Southern University A&M College, a HBCU institution. Consequently, because of its proximity to Southern, the primary residents in this oasis were administrators, professors and athletic personnel affiliated with Southern.[8]

Success Is Contagious

I grew up in the same neighborhood as the first African American to earn a Ph.D. in mathematics from Louisiana State University (LSU) and the first female to serve as Chancellor of both Southern University campuses, Dr. Dolores Spikes. In addition to Dr. Spikes, PV was home to legendary SU Director of Bands, Dr. Isaac Greggs, and legendary SU Professors Dr. Oscar Mitchell and Dr. Augustus Blanks. One of the most respected trainers in college athletics, SU Head Athletic Trainer Carl Williams, and one the most decorated high school football coaches in Louisiana, SU Laboratory School Head Football Coach Carl Porter, both lived down the street from us.

---

[8] Park Vista was so close to SU, my neighborhood friends and I attended summer camp on SU's campus. At camp, we learned how to use a bow and arrow, swim, play tennis, run track and play basketball – valuable skills for a kid in the 70s.

Dr. Press Robinson   *Robert Jones*

We also lived around the corner from legendary leaders like Dr. Press Robinson, the first African American elected to the East Baton Rouge Parish School Board and its first African American president. Dr. Robinson would go on to become the Chancellor of Southern University at New Orleans. My godfather, Robert Jones, a former SU Board Member and elementary school principal, called PV home as well. PV was home to numerous award-winning athletes: Tracy Porter, Leroy and Leroyal Jones, Reginald Jones, Karl Wilson, Cleve Baily, Charles Brown, Roderick White, Kevin Poydras and Adrian Stacy. Moreover, PV was filled with some of the most talented, traffic-stopping beauties on the planet: Michelle Davis, Deidra Marcell, Cathy Williams, Renee Scott, Edwill Jacobs, Jacentha Buggs, Wanda Page, Rose Hudson, Rhonda Spikes, Bernice Jordan, Rholanda Malveaux and Valencia DeCuir. Additonally, PV was home to award winning journalists Don Lemon and the late Ed Buggs. And numerous elected officials, high school principals, teachers, doctors, lawyers and African American business owners called Park Vista home as well.

Church Fathers

Pastor Charles T. Smith

In addition to growing up in an all-black neighborhood, I attended an all-black church – Shiloh Missionary Baptist Church, pastored by the late great Reverend Charles T. Smith. At Shiloh, Pastor Smith cultivated a nurturing environment built on love and mutual respect. As a child, I always felt loved and appreciated at Shiloh. Pastor Smith, his lovely wife, the beloved Stoney Smith, the deacons and the deaconesses always made all the kids feel very special and needed. We all enjoyed going to Sunday school, vacation bible school and Sunday morning services. Hence, participation in the youth choir and other youth activities was always high. Because of this, my churchmates and I grew up with a great appreciation and reverence for Jesus Christ and respect for our parents, the elderly and people in authority. While attending Shiloh, I accepted Jesus Christ as my personal savior, sang my first solo, gave my first speech and acted in my first play.

Additionally, when I was in high school, my dad introduced me to Atty. Brace Godfrey, a member of Shiloh MBC, who would soon become my first "attorney" role model. After meeting Brace and spending time with him, I was 100% sure that I wanted to be an attorney, but not just any attorney, I wanted to be an attorney like Brace: respected by my peers; the husband of a beautiful wife; the patriarch of a beautiful family; with a warrior like spirit cloaked in humility and kindness.[9] To me, Shiloh was and remains a special place! Thanks Pastor Smith!

Guard Your Eyes

Thanks to the fathers in my neighborhood and at church, I grew up very confident *in* my skin and *with* my skin. I didn't know many of my

---

[9] Atty Brace Godfrey was a generational leader. After learning about his sudden and unexpected passing, like many, I mourned his loss for months. Fortunately for me, prior to Brace's death, I developed a close relationship with his son, Trey. Thankfully, Trey has embraced his dad's legacy and is building on the foundation that his father established.

"neighborhood fathers" very well; I knew them through my parents or from observing them from afar. However, hearing my parents brag about our neighbors and observing them on a regular basis was all the motivation I needed to dream and dream big! In fact, nearly all of the positive interactions that I had with people outside of my family were with people of my own race. The only place where I consistently saw negative images of black people was on television. Thankfully, I grew up at a time when playing outdoors was the thing to do, so except for watching competitive sports, I didn't watch much TV.

School Fathers

I attended an all-black kindergarten, Rev. James Kindergarten School – named after the pastor of the First Presbyterian Church of Scotlandville. After graduating from kindergarten (as valedictorian), I attended an all-black elementary school, Progress Elementary, for three years. In third grade, however, because of forced busing, I began attending Baker Field, a predominantly white public school. Until then, I had never been particularly close to or comfortable around any non–African Americans. This was probably because my parents, and all their friends, came of age in a segregated South, and none of them had many non–African American friends or associates. The only white person I felt relatively close to was local TV personality William P. "Buckskin Bill" Black, whom I watched every morning before school. All my friends and I loved watching the Buckskin Bill Show and Storyland, especially the Monday Morning March.

My life changed forever when my third-grade teacher at Baker Field sent me home with a letter addressed to my parents written in red ink. The two-page note complained about my classroom behavior. The teacher was not fond of me or my childhood best friend, Darryl Robertson, especially when we pretended to be members of the Black Panther Party.[10] Needless to say, when I arrived home with the note, my parents were very unhappy with me; surprisingly, though, they were also unhappy with my teacher. My dad always had one rule when it came to school: the teacher is *always* right! But in this case, he couldn't get over the fact that the letter was written in red ink, and that the teacher was treating Darryl and me as if we were grown men and not third-graders. My parents didn't believe her characterization of my behavior, and being teachers themselves, they understood the impact a teacher could have on a student's self-esteem and self-worth. Two years later, they would transfer me to St. Anthony, a Catholic school. However, before I left Baker Field, my dad challenged me to change that teacher's

---

[10] Darryl Robertson was a loyal and committed friend to many, but especially to me. He was truly the "best" best friend any kid could ever have. We did everything together, and we stayed very close for years. Both of us cared a lot about our community and believed we could make a difference by becoming lawyers. However, Darryl did much more than become an attorney. He was the first community activist I ever got to know on a personal basis. Though he departed this life unexpectedly, he left a mark that will never be erased.

beliefs about me! He also told me to do my best to impress all my teachers and to make them smile, not just my classmates.

St. Anthony School

Patrick Reine

Show Love

The transition to St. Anthony was very difficult. I began playing organized football and basketball for the first time, and to my surprise, I excelled athletically. But my grades were terrible. My academic woes persisted until I came to know Patrick Reine and Rev. Alfred J. LaFleur. From our very first meeting Mr. Reine, an Air Force veteran, treated me as if I were his very own son. Every day, he would encourage me to be the best and do my best, not only in sports but also in the classroom. I do not remember a day when Mr. Reine didn't have an encouraging word to say to me. I still don't know why he treated me the way he did, but he wasn't alone; his wife Alice, an administrator at St. Anthony; Mrs. Reine's niece, Ms. Smith, who was one of my teachers; his son Chris, my basketball coach; and his daughters, who attended school with me, all treated me like family. This was the case even though before becoming a student at St. Anthony, neither I nor my parents had ever even heard of Mr. Reine. To me, the Reines were like angels sent down from heaven! God is truly amazing!

While I attended St. Anthony, Mr. Reine was an assistant basketball and football coach. Under his guidance and that of his son Chris, the Head Basketball Coach, I won every award imaginable in basketball, and I was also "that dude" in football. High school coaches regularly attended my junior high football and basketball games. As soon as my parents started getting to know Mr. Reine, they knew they made the right decision enrolling me at St. Anthony.

Father LaFleur

Mr. Reine was a devout Catholic, and he introduced me to the parish priest, Rev. Alfred Joseph LaFleur. Father LaFleur was more than a priest; he was a scholar and a former teacher. It was clear that he cared about the students at St. Anthony and that he loved his role as parish priest. Even though I was a non-Catholic, Father LaFleur would let me help my Catholic classmates prepare for the school's weekly mass. He even allowed me to perform certain duties during mass that were designated for altar boys only, like ringing the bells during the sacred part of the service, the Eucharist or transubstantiation.

Goodness Is Not Relegated to a Race or a Religion

At St. Anthony, taking religion classes and attending weekly services were mandatory. These required religious experiences, coupled with my participation in organized sports, imperceptibly and subconsciously enabled me to incorporate the teachings of Christ that I'd first learned at home and at Shiloh into my everyday life. Mr. Reine and Father LeFleur were the first non–African American men that I developed a close bond with. It was because of them that I decided, in eighth grade, that I really wanted to be like Jesus – not just at home or at church, but in life and for life. And it was because of my relationship with Coach Reine and Father LeFleur that, nearly ten years after the assassination of civil rights icon Martin Luther King, Jr., I stopped making snap judgments about people based on the color of their skin – or, as my dad would often say, their "body bag." I even realized that God not only created good Baptists, God also created good Catholics! LOL

Worth noting, when I was about to graduate from high school, Mr. Reine called my parents and told them that St. Anthony's administrative staff had decided to retire my football and basketball jerseys. Needless to say, my entire family was in disbelief! We were blown away! But that's not all. At the jersey retirement banquet held in my honor, Mr. Reine somehow managed to get the Head Football Coach at LSU, Jerry Stovall, to be the keynote speaker. Also worth noting, not only was Mr. Reine a devout Catholic, he was a graduate of Catholic High School of Baton Rouge (CHS) and a lover of all things CHS and LSU. Thus, to no one's surprise, after graduating from St. Anthony I attended CHS and eventually signed an athletic scholarship agreement to play football at LSU. As a final note and as discussed below, Coach Reine not only introduced me to Father LaFleur, he introduced me to CHS track and field coach Pete Boudreaux! Besides my own dad, Mr. Reine was "that dude" in my life.

Catholic High School

Background

Catholic High School was and still is an all-boys parochial school that's highly regarded as one the best college and life preparatory schools in the country. During my time there, CHS was administered by the Brothers of the Sacred Heart. The Brothers served as the school's principals, teachers and disciplinarians. Thus, with the exception of my typing and French teacher, all of my teachers were men and most of them "brothers." There was not a large female presence on campus, and corporeal punishment was an acceptable and expected method to deter classroom misbehavior and school rule infractions.

When I attended CHS there were fewer than 50 African Americans students in the entire school. In fact, there were only five black students in my freshmen class: Maurice Coleman (a Grizzly Great), Herff Jones (an honors graduate), Robert Nobles (a Grizzly Great) and Eric Roquemore (a standout in football), and of course me. The only other African Americans at the school were the Director of Choirs, Dr. Vickie Lott, the janitors and members of the cafeteria staff. But this didn't phase me one iota. My attitude regarding race, as discussed above, was honed as a result of growing up in a positive black environment. I didn't have a self-esteem problem, I didn't believe I had to prove myself to anyone, or vice versa, and I didn't believe that any person (black or white, male or female) was intrinsically better than anyone else. And because of my relationship with Mr. Reine and Father LaFleur, I knew that kindness and goodness were not determined by a person's "body bag." Nevertheless, prior to enrolling at CHS, I didn't actually want to go there. None of my close friends went to CHS, it was an all-boys school, and academic success was not guaranteed, even if you studied. I was scared to death that I wouldn't be able to compete academically.[11]

---

[11] My fears were soon allayed after a 10-minute conversation with Ms. Smith, Alice Reine's niece. Ms. Smith was my eighth-grade social studies teacher at St. Anthony. A few days before the end of the school year, she asked me if I was worried about doing well academically at CHS. I told her yes. At that point, she looked me straight in my eyes, without blinking, and told me in no uncertain terms that I had the ability to make all A's at CHS. She "made" me believe in myself. After my first semester in ninth grade, I went back to St. Anthony and showed Ms. Smith my report card – I made all A's.

Discipline and Preparation

The most revered and feared figure on the CHS campus was Brother Gordian Udinsky, S.C. He was revered because he was a well-regarded scholar who'd dedicated most of his adult life to teaching high school boys science and physics. He was feared because he stood at least 6 foot 5, weighed over 250 pounds, had a baritone voice and demanded absolute order and obedience in his classroom. And that's not all. Every student had to be perfectly groomed and neatly dressed when entering his class and prepared to read a section of that day's lesson out loud while standing up. No excuses were acceptable or accepted. If a student read a particular section incorrectly or failed to properly enunciate a word, that student would remain standing for the entire class.[12] When Bro. Gordian made a sound or uttered a word, every student was required to discontinue all activities immediately and fasten his eyes on Bro. Gordian. If not, discipline was swift and memorable!

In my freshman year, Brother Gordian was my Earth and Space Science teacher. Like all my classmates, at first, I feared him. Stories about Bro. Gordian's unwavering demands were told not only during lunch hour at junior high cafeterias across Baton Rouge, but also at campsites late at night while roasting marshmallows around the campfire. However, like many of my classmates, the more I got to know Bro. Gordian, the more I respected him. He taught us about a universe that was perfectly ordered and disciplined and thus, in his own way, he taught us about "the other side" of God. Most of us only knew about God from the perspective of Jesus Christ as the Lamb of God. However, in Brother Gordian's class I discovered that God was not just "love" but also "science!" I learned that God truly holds the whole world in His hands – and me too. Being in Bro. Gordian's class helped me understand that much of my capabilities and potential could only be realized through properly preparing myself for the task at hand.

Encouragement Can Change a Life

Around the end of my first semester in his class, out of nowhere, Bro. Gordian asked if he could speak with me privately. Of course, I said "Yes sir." Once my classmates had left the room, Brother Gordian said he'd heard I was a pretty good football player and that, at least in his class (he laughed), I was a good student. Then he told me he was proud of me and to keep up the good work. Needless to say, hearing those words from "Big G" set me on fire! From that point on, I gave CHS all I had to offer.

While at CHS, I became the lead liturgy singer for nearly all religious services. I ran for several student government offices and was elected student council treasurer and secretary in consecutive years. I became a member of the National Honor Society and was a founding

---

[12] At the time, I didn't know that Brother Gordian was preparing me for law school and the Socratic method.

member of CHS' Fellowship of Christian Athletes "Huddle."[13] I received All State honors as a member of the CHS choir – like Big G, I sang baritone. I also received numerous MVP awards in football and track and set or was a part of setting numerous school, district and parish records in both sports and one state record in track and field. In fact, in 1982, in football, I was named MVP of our district, MVP of the City of Baton Rouge and MVP of East Baton Rouge Parish, and I was the first recipient of WBRZ's Offensive Player of the Year Award. I was named one of the top ten graduates of my senior class, and several years later, I became the first African American football player to be inducted into CHS' Grizzly Greats Hall of Fame. I was able to accomplish all of the above simply because God placed "fathers" in my life who believed in me and encouraged me to believe in myself. Brother Gordian may have been my first "CHS Father," but he most definitely was not the last. Another man at CHS who caused me to "level up" was Coach Pete Boudreaux, affectionately known as Coach Boo.[14] Because of Coach Boo, the phrase "I can't" was completely removed from my heart and mind.

---

[13] CHS Head Baseball Coach and Assistant Football Coach Gerry Garidel was responsible for establishing the FCA Huddle Chapter at CHS and getting me involved with organization. I have been intimately nvolved with FCA ever since. Thanks Coach.

[14] Coach Boudreaux is one of the most decorated high school track and field coaches in America. While at CHS, Coach Boudreaux led his teams to 18 state cross-country championships, 14 state indoor track titles and 18 state outdoor track championships. In 2016, Coach Boo was inducted into the National High School Hall of Fame, and he was selected by the U.S. Track & Field and Cross-Country Coaches Association as the Boys' Coach of the Year for the state of Louisiana. He's also a member of the Louisiana Sports Hall of Fame. CHS honored Coach's legacy in 2017 by dedicating its track and field facility in his honor – The Pete Boudreaux Track.

Coach Pete Boudreaux

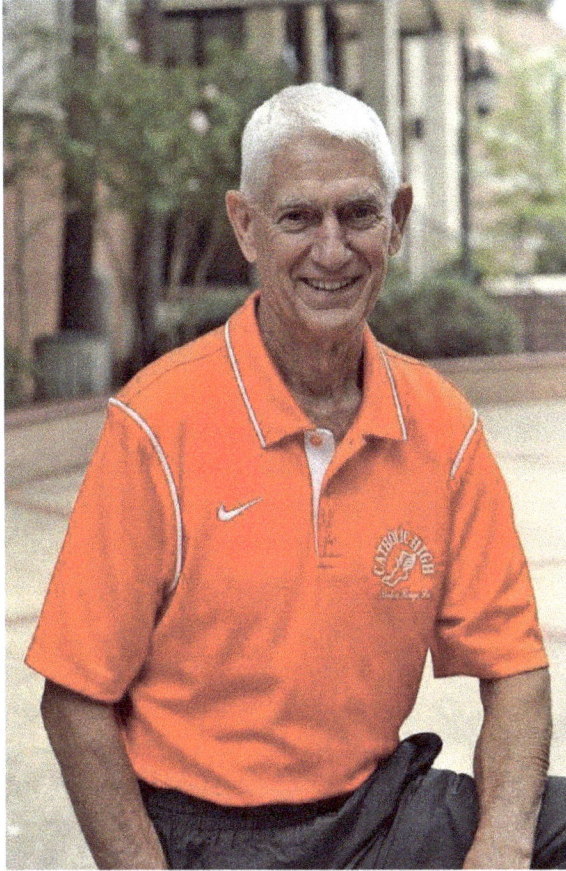

Background

When I enrolled at CHS, Coach Boudreaux was the Athletic Director. He was also the Head Cross-Country and Track and Field Coach. I was a member of the track and field team, but until my sophomore year in high school, I had never run a race longer than 200 meters.[15] I had stuck with the 100- and 200-meter dashes and the 4x100-meter relay, and because I won most of my individual races, I was content. However, on one fateful day one of my teammates was injured, and Coach Boo asked me to do

---

[15] As mentioned above, Coach Reine introduced me to Coach Boudreaux. While I was attending St. Anthony, Coach Reine encouraged me to run track during the summer months. At the time, Coach Boudreaux coached the Red Stick Striders Track and Field team. I joined the track team and ran track for Red Stick for at least two summers while in junior high school.

something I'd never done before: run the final leg of CHS' 4x400-meter relay. I didn't want to do it, nor did I think I could. I told Coach Boo, "No sir!" I told him, "I can't." I explained that I was too muscular and my thigh muscles were too big to run that fast for that long. My teammates laughed. Coach Boo did too.

Every day for weeks, Coach Boo asked me the same question, and every day I gave him the same answer: "No sir!" To make me feel guilty, Coach would wait to ask me until I was around my teammates. Still, I always said, "Coach, if I could, I would. But since I can't, I ain't!" But Coach never gave up. Soon I was hiding from Coach Boudreaux at the beginning and end of each track practice. Finally, one day, after being cornered by my teammates, I gave in and agreed to join the mile relay team. The other three guys on the team were CHS greats Neal Dellocono (the Italian Stallion); Robert Nobles (the Gapper) and Stewart Eames (the Lapper).

Never Say "I Can't"

Training for the mile relay was brutal. After Coach's famed 60-second all-out runs, I either threw up or cramped up. But no matter my condition, Coach Boo and my teammates constantly encouraged me and pushed me. Eventually, my 400-meter split time was consistently between 49 and 51 seconds. I might add, this was the slowest split on the team (because of my muscular legs, of course).

Eventually, however, as Coach Boo had predicted, the more comfortable I became with running 400 meters, the more the CHS mile relay team became the topic of discussion all over the state of Louisiana. We won, and we won big. In nearly every race, Neal (the Stallion) would hand off the baton to Robert, usually with a 10- to 30-yard lead. Robert (the Gapper) would extend the lead by an additional 50 to 100 yards, and Stew (the Lapper) would usually lap the team in last place prior to handing the baton off to me. All I was asked to do was run my race and avoid disqualification. I followed the script until the 1980 State Track and Field Championship at LSU's Bernie Moore Track Stadium.

The mile relay is the last event at every track meet. It's one of the few track events where speed, endurance and having a running strategy are all instrumental in the outcome. At the 1980 State Track and Field

Championship, like at nearly every track meet, the stands were packed with people waiting to see the final event. Prior to running the relay, we were all nervous. Nevertheless, just like in our last ten races, Neal, Robert and Stewart did what was expected. When Stew handed the baton to me, I had at least a 50-yard lead on the second-place team from Leesville, Louisiana. However, when I rounded the final curve for the home stretch, I saw something in my peripheral vision that I'd never witnessed before. Everyone in the bleachers was standing. I couldn't hear anything, but it looked like they were all yelling and screaming. Then all of a sudden, for the first time, I felt someone behind me. Instead of running my race, I panicked. I tightened up and lost all running form. Then the unthinkable happened. At about 10 yards from the finish line, the anchor leg for Leesville High School passed me up as if I was standing still. I lost the race!

After crossing the finish line, I kept running towards the turf-covered inner field, where I fell to the ground. I was devastated. I was embarrassed. I was humiliated. I wanted to run away. But I couldn't. I was too tired. How could I lose with a 50-yard lead? How? I was inconsolable. However, 30 or so minutes after I collapsed, through my disgust and hurt, I heard a state track meet official speaking over the loudspeakers. He began announcing the point totals for each team. When he announced the totals for the teams competing for the AAA state title – which included CHS – the CHS faithful jumped and began shouting uncontrollably. Although our mile relay team had finished in second place, CHS won its first outdoor state title in track and field in school history.

Almost immediately, Coach Boo and my teammates piled on top of me and started congratulating me and thanking me for making the sacrifice to join the mile relay team. Coach and the others told me that if I hadn't joined the team, CHS might not have won state! Needless to say, I felt much better. I was no longer exhausted, nor did I want to leave the stadium. I began celebrating with my teammates and the CHS faithful, the people who attended every track meet throughout the season. Though my "boyz" have never let me forget "DA RACE," that race has constantly reminded me that you can lose an event and still win a title! To my complete shock, later that year at the spring sports convocation, Coach Boo and my teammates named me the 1980 MVP for track and field. I was overwhelmed!

Next year, at the 1981 State Track Meet, CHS again won the outdoor title, and the mile relay team, consisting of the same fellas, set a Louisiana state mile relay record that stood for over 35 years. As a result, when it comes to a challenge, I have never uttered the phrase "I can't" ever again.

Coach Curtis Varnado

In addition to running track, I played football for all four years at CHS as a running back. In my freshman year, I broke every freshman rushing record in school history. As a sophomore, I had a few memorable games, although I missed several due to a shoulder injury. As a junior, senior running back Neal Dellocono and I rushed for nearly 1000 yards each. In the fall of 1981, my last football season at CHS, behind a veteran offensive line led by Eric Roquemore, Greg Polozola, Lurry Lacour, Brian Wampold, Rick Tuminello and Jimbo Dantin, I rushed for over 1500 yards and scored nearly 20 touchdowns, all school records. Truth be told, I could have rushed for more than 2000 yards and scored 30 touchdowns. However, in several games when we were winning by two or more touchdowns, CHS Head Football Coach Curtis Varnado (Coach V) would not allow me and several other members of the offensive line to play the entire game. Though I was disappointed with the lost opportunity to set state records for yards rushed and touchdowns scored, Coach V taught me and my teammates two valuable life lessons that season about sportsmanship and character.

Regarding sportsmanship, Coach V reminded the team that the goal in any game is to win, not to demoralize your opponent. Regarding character, he routinely stated that a man's character is revealed in how he handles the spoils of victory and deals with the agony of defeat. According to Coach V, "Everybody gets a turn to ride the Ferris wheel of life." Thus, he reminded us to always win with class and lose with class. I've carried those lessons with me every day, especially since becoming an attorney.

My College Fathers

Background

During the fall of 1981 and the spring of 1982, my senior year in high school, I was heavily recruited to play football by several universities across the country. College coaches were on campus almost every day. Local media outlets were regularly asking me to give a statement about the recruiting process. From December to February, I made several official visits to various universities, trying to decide which to attend. Because Duke University reminded me of the environment at CHS, I initially made a verbal commitment to attend Duke. Ultimately, however, I accepted a scholarship offer to play football at LSU. This was because LSU was my mom's choice and because I genuinely liked Head Coach Jerry Stovall.[16] And so, in the fall of 1982, I became a Tiger. I also became part of what was arguably the greatest group of running backs to ever play for the Tigers. Every one of those running backs would go on to play football in the NFL.

Before the start of on-the-field practices, all the freshmen were put through a series of drills that tested our speed, quickness, agility, reaction time, jumping ability, and strength. Because of my performance, a day or two after the "testing" ended, on the front page of the sports section of one of the local papers, there was a picture of me under the headline "Superman Has Arrived on Campus." Needless to say, I was thrilled. However, when on-the-field practices began, I was in a fierce battle with Dalton Hillard and Gary James for the starting tailback position. We were being evaluated on every play. Everybody was giving it their all. Dalton had moves and balance that no one had ever seen before, and Gary had the speed and power to rival any NFL running back. I, on the other hand, had more speed than Dalton and I could out-"shake" Gary. The battle was fierce – until I fractured two ribs.

---

[16] Coach Jerry Stovall, prior to becoming the Head Football Coach at LSU, was a much-accomplished college and professional football player. He was a unanimous selection to the 1962 College Football All-America Team, selected to the NFL Pro Bowl in 1966, 1967 and 1969, and, in 2010, Coach Stovall was inducted into the College Football Hall of Fame.

I was asked to run a post route during passing drills. The ball was overthrown, but I laid out for the ball anyway. When I did, a defensive back, who will remain nameless (LOL!), hit me in my rib cage. And so when the season started, I was rehabbing my injury, and Dalton and Gary took the SEC by storm. Coach Stovall decided to redshirt me so that I could fully heal from my injury and gain an extra year of eligibility.

Before my next football season, because Dalton and Gary had solidified themselves at the tailback position, I made the decision to move to fullback. I put on an additional 15 pounds and worked on my run blocking skills. I looked like an SEC fullback, but it took me a while to feel like one. Slowly but surely, the change from tailback to fullback happened, not only in my body, but eventually in my heart and mind. I started to enjoy playing fullback, especially if it meant that I would get a chance to play a lot during the games.

Coach Stovall

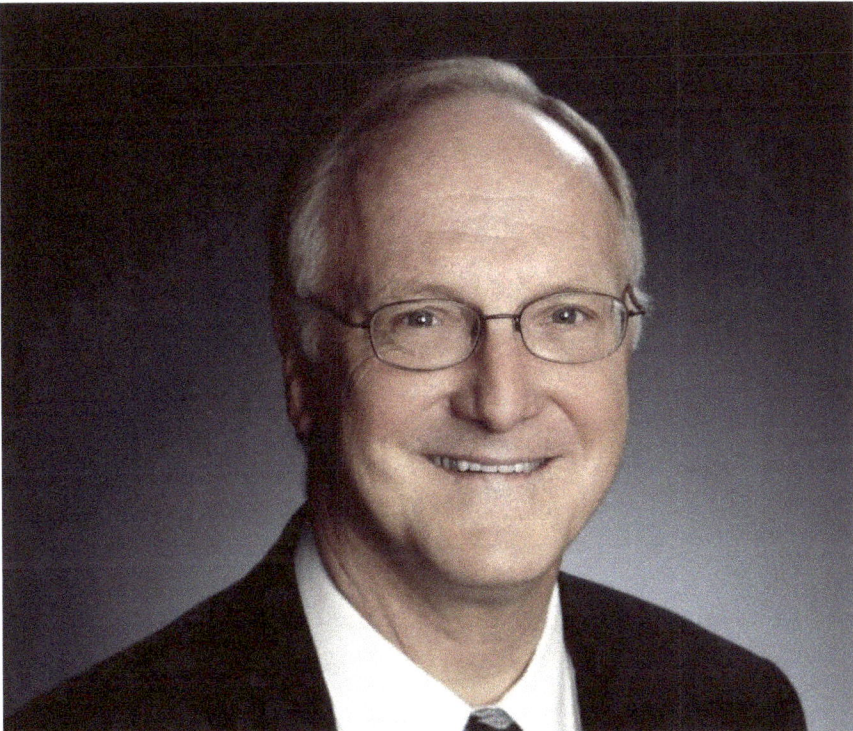

Freedom to Make a Mistake

Right after the transition, I started practicing with the third-string offense. Before long, however, I was practicing with the first- and second-string offense, alternating with Gene Lang, the starting fullback and one of the best teammates I ever had. Though I was alternating with Geno, my practice performance didn't translate into significant playing time on game day. As a result, I had a meeting with my position coach to discuss the situation. He told me to be patient. I decided to wait until the second half of the season to see if things would change. Nothing did. Then, during a routine mid-week practice, my position coach made a joke about me not getting in the game. It was the kind of joke that caused some of the other running backs to turn and look at me to see how I would respond. I didn't, verbally. But mentally, I was done. I was majoring in Petroleum Engineering, and I decided to leave the team before the end of the 1983 season and focus on my studies.

I spoke with my parents. They were upset. I spoke with LSU Head Coach Jerry Stovall. He was upset. Coach Stovall wanted to meet with me and my parents. We met.

During the meeting, I told Coach Stovall everything. We all cried in his office, and he asked me to take a few days off and reconsider. I indicated that because of what had happened and what was said, I didn't think I could be coached by my position coach anymore. Though my parents and Coach Stovall could have done some things to make it extremely difficult, if not impossible, for me to leave LSU, they let me turn in my gear and leave the team. Looking back, leaving LSU was not a good choice. Nevertheless, to this day, I appreciate Coach Stovall for letting me do what I believed I needed to do. Coach Stovall gave me the freedom to make a mistake! I can honestly say that I've learned just as much, if not more, from the mistakes I've made in life than from any "right" decision that I've made.

Worth mentioning, after the 1983 football season and before I'd decided to transfer to another university, then LSU Athletic Director Bob Broadhead terminated Coach Stovall's contract and hired Bill Arnsparger as LSU's next Head Football Coach. Shortly thereafter, I received a phone call from one of Director Broadhead's associate Athletic Directors. He asked me to reconsider my decision to leave the team now that Coach Stovall had been replaced, but I declined – I didn't want anyone to think I'd left the team because of Coach Stovall. Looking back, that was probably another mistake.

Significantly, my decision to transfer to another university was probably one of the lowest points of my life. I couldn't go anywhere in Baton Rouge without being bombarded with questions about my decision. It was the topic of discussion on TV, on the radio and in the paper. Out of concern for my mental health, my dad encouraged me to speak with the late Judge Frank Polozola, former US District Judge of the US District Court for the Middle District of Louisiana and CHS alumnus. My Dad and Judge Polozola had gotten to know one another because Judge Polozola's son, Greg, and I were good friends and played football together at CHS. My dad hoped that Judge Polozola would say something to help me get through this period in my life. My dad was right.

Several weeks after leaving Coach Stovall's office, I received a phone call from Judge Polozola's administrative assistant inviting me to visit with the Judge in his chambers at the Middle District Court House. When I arrived for my appointment, Judge Polozola was "on the bench" listening to two lawyers "argue" their respective positions in an effort to convince him to rule in their favor. To my shock, when I walked into his court room, he immediately acknowledged my presence and introduced me to the attorneys standing before him. After the lawyers completed their arguments, Judge Polozola announced his ruling and court was adjourned. He then invited me into his chambers.

I sat down in a chair in front of his desk. The Judge began the conversation by reminding me of the success I had at CHS. Then he asked if I was able to follow what had just happened in court. I said "yes." He explained to me that the decision he made was not easy, but he had to make a decision – he had to rule - and that after he ruled, even though one of the attorneys agreed with his decision and the other did not, court was immediately adjourned and he moved on to the next matter, his meeting with me. At that point in the conversation, I got the point. Realizing that I understood what he was saying, Judge Polozola shook my hand, gave me a "bear" hug and wished me well in all my endeavors. I was ready to move forward.

USL I

Background

In January 1984, I transferred to the University of Southwestern Louisiana in Lafayette. I chose USL because I wanted to play football again, and because I was majoring in Petroleum Engineering and USL had one of the most respected petroleum engineering departments in the country. Additionally, I wanted to work in the oil industry, and Lafayette was home to numerous oil companies and industry partners.

Soon after moving onto USL's campus and hanging out around the football practice fields and the student union, I realized that I didn't know many people at USL. Even though I'd just made one of the biggest decisions in my life, there was no one on campus or on the football team I could really talk to. Plus, because of NCAA transfer rules, I wasn't allowed to participate in any football-related activities. 1984 was the first year since fifth grade that I hadn't played football. Each day was filled with hours of no one telling me where to go or what to do. For the first time, I was a "real" college student. Unfortunately, I didn't know how to manage my time without sports; fall 1984 was my worst academic semester ever, and I was placed on academic probation.

The next year, 1985, was not much better academically or athletically. Even though my grades improved and I became eligible to play football, I severely injured my right ankle on an underground sprinkler head during the first game of the 1985 football season. It was a high ankle sprain, and it was so severe that I didn't play again the rest of the season. At this point, any dream I had of playing professionally looked extremely bleak. According to NCAA guidelines, a student athlete has five calendar years to play 4 seasons in a sport. The 1986 season represented my fifth year in college and thus my final year of eligibility.

At the conclusion of the 1985 football season, because I hadn't made any notable contribution in a college game since my second season at LSU, I was listed third on the depth chart at the running back position. This meant that the likelihood of me seeing any significant playing time was dependent upon someone ahead of me getting injured. Needless to say, I was not too optimistic about my chances of playing during my senior season – much less getting an opportunity to play at the next level. Then there was a change in leadership.

Barry Wilson

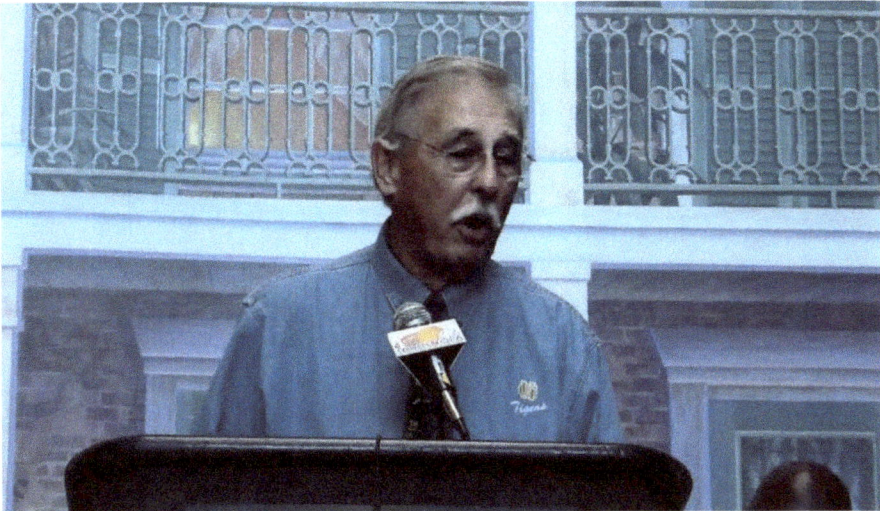

Not long after the end of the 1985 football season, USL's Athletic Director fired the entire football coaching staff and hired Nelson Stokely as Head Football Coach. Coach Stokely, soon after being hired, named Barry Wilson as the team's Offensive Coordinator.[17] Once he had hired his

---

[17] Prior to becoming a coach at the collegiate level, Coach Barry Wilson was a member of the Holy Cross (in New Orleans) 1963 State Championship Football Team and a high school All-American. He played football at LSU, where he was an All-SEC offensive lineman and was voted captain of the 1967 LSU football team. After coaching college

assistant coaches, Coach Stokely and his assistants met with the whole team. After the team meeting, each coach met one on one with every player he was expected to coach. When it was my turn to meet with Coach Wilson, he told me he was very familiar with my ability to play football and with the injuries I'd sustained earlier in my college career. He also told me he was going to install a "run-n-shoot" style offense and that he wanted me to play the wingback/slot position. Then, seemingly out of nowhere, Coach Wilson told me that he believed in me and that I would be first on the depth chart at the slot position! I was so excited about the opportunity, I hurriedly shook his hand and told him that he did not make a mistake and that I would make him proud. I left his office on cloud nine and immediately started preparing myself for the upcoming year.

Coach Wilson's run-n-shoot offense was a godsend to me. The offense showcased my ability to catch the football and to run in open space. As fate would have it, during the 1986 season, I not only played in every game, I set a new USL receiving and yardage record for running backs. As a result, I found out that my name was on the draft board for several NFL teams. However, when the 1986 season ended, I wasn't invited to play in any College Allstar Bowl games, nor was I invited to participate in the NFL combine leading up to the 1987 NFL Draft. Nevertheless, because of my success during the 1986 season, I not only wanted to play on the next level, I knew I could.

So instead of waiting around for an NFL team to call, I started participating in every professional football workout and tryout event in and around Louisiana, mainly those sponsored by the Canadian Football League (CFL). Whether the tryout was located in Houston, Texas; Ruston, Louisiana; New Orleans, Louisiana; or Jackson, Mississippi, I did my best to impress every scout I came in contact with. I was consistently a top performer at every tryout, however, I never got a call back. Then lightning struck.

---

football for several years, Coach Wilson returned to his high school alma mater, serving as the Head Football Coach for Holy Cross from 2002-2014 and later becoming the school's Athletic Director.

At the conclusion of the 1986 football season, my teammate, defensive back Elton Slater, was considered one of the top-rated defensive backs in the country. He was also an outstanding track athlete. So, of course, the NFL scouts were "blowing up" his phone leading up to the 1987 Draft. A month or so before draft day, I was getting ready for bed when I heard a knock on my dorm room door. Although, my roommate, R.C. "Big City" Mullen, was standing closest to the door, "told" me to answer it. Big City was 6 feet 7 inches tall and weighed 300 pounds. So, I immediately got up and answered the door! (LOL) When I opened it, Elton was standing in the hallway. He told me that an NFL scout was coming to the school the next day to work him out, and he wondered if I would work out with him. Of course I said yes. He told me thanks and said that this could be big for both of us and to meet him at Bourgeois Hall, USL's indoor track and field facility, around noon. Note that Elton could have asked any senior on the entire team to work out with him. But he asked me! Like Coach Wilson, Elton believed in me and wanted to give me an opportunity to show what I could do. Worth noting, at that time, the NFL would send area scouts to schools that didn't have a history of producing many NFL-caliber players. Thus, though only one scout would attend a given workout, that scout was responsible for reporting the results of the workout to all NFL teams.

Needless to say, after Elton left, I couldn't sleep. I tossed and turned most of the night, full of anxiety and excitement. I called my parents. I called my girlfriend. I prayed and prayed and prayed. Eventually, I fell asleep. When I woke up the next morning, I hurriedly made my way to Bourgeois Hall. I was two hours early. I jogged. I stretched. I worked on my start. I practiced the expected agility drills. I was ready. But surprisingly, I wasn't nervous. Then it dawned on me why. It was because of the CFL tryouts! I immediately began to thank God. Because I'd never gotten a call back after a tryout, I thought that all the time and money spent and all the miles I put on my car were wasted. I was wrong.

When the NFL scout arrived, I immediately went to the locker room and prayed. I asked God to please make my feet run faster than they'd ever run before. In Jesus name! He answered my prayer. Elton was up first. As expected, Elton ran well. His time in the 40-yard dash was 4.4 seconds. I was up next. Once I'd completed the 40-yard dash, the scout asked me to run again. I did. Apparently, my second 40, in terms of time, was the same as the first. I asked if I needed to run a third time. The scout said no. Then he told me that I'd run the 40 in 4.3 seconds, twice. I was overwhelmed!

The next day, my phone rang off the hook. Seven NFL teams called me and asked about my health, my family, my dreams and if I wanted to travel to see their facilities. I was being recruited all over again. I expected – and wanted – to be drafted. However, my name wasn't called during the 1987 NFL Draft.[18] Instead, I was considered a high-priority free agent. That meant that immediately after the draft, several NFL teams

---

[18] As it turned out, I wasn't drafted because I didn't know how to play the "draft game." Several teams started calling me after the conclusion of the fourth round. Every time a team called, I answered the phone and engaged in a five-minute conversation with a team representative. I didn't know that I needed to be "unavailable," i.e., that I needed someone else to answer my phone and indicate that I was on another line talking to another team. Because I was always available, each team that called me assumed that their team was the only team interested in me. Thus, each team that contacted me assumed that they could possibly sign me as a free agent and use their draft pick on a more "sought-after" player.

offered me contracts to play professionally as a running back. I eventually accepted an offer to play running back with the Detroit Lions. After participating in training camp and playing in four preseason games, when the Lions' final roster was published, my name was on the list. I was the only rookie free agent to make the Lions 1987 active roster and the only rookie free agent to become a starter. All of this was possible because two people believed in me: Coach Barry Wilson and Elton Slater.[19] In response to their immeasurable contribution to my life, I have and will continue to pay it forward for the rest of my life!!! Like Coach Wilson and Elton, I also take calculated risks on the people that I'm in relationship with.

The NFL

As mentioned above, my NFL career was cut short due to a knee injury suffered during my second year. The injury was so severe that when the Lions' head athletic trainer notified the hospital about me he concluded his remarks by saying "Possible amputee."[20] However, prior to my injury, I was fortunate to have experienced a few career highlights.

The first highlight came in 1987, my rookie season, when the Lions played the Washington Redskins (now called the Washington Commanders). At the start of the game, I was second on the depth chart at the tailback position. By the end of the game, I was the starting tailback! Though I didn't have a 100-yard game, I scored my first NFL touchdown and I – with the help of my teammates – was able to show the world that I could *run dat ball*! Former NFL Head Coach and Hall of Fame inductee Dick Vermeil was one of the television analysts for the game. The commentary Coach Vermeil provided on my ability to run with the ball and to create lanes to run through put the league on notice.

My second career highlight also came in 1987, when the Lions played the Kansas City Chiefs on Thanksgiving Day. That game, an NFL tradition dating back to 1934, was nationally televised. I rushed for 100 yards, had over 50 yards receiving and scored a touchdown. My parents were in the stands watching me play – their first time seeing me play as a professional athlete in person. However, based on the number of phone

---

[19] Sadly, on February 15, 2022, Elton died in a car accident in Port Arthur, Texas. But rest assured, I will always tell the story of how I made it to the league. Thanks E!

[20] Special thanks to the Lions' trainers and team physicians and the medical staff at Henry Ford Hospital in Detroit Michigan for the exemplary care they provided. Although I was unable to play professional football again, I was and am still able to fully engage in activities that help make this life worth living.

calls I got, every living soul who knew me or had heard of me saw the game. My phone rang nonstop for two days. I received commercial opportunities and was a requested guest speaker and singer for several organizations in and around Detroit, including the Detroit Pistons. To this day, many of my friends and family still talk about that game as if it was televised yesterday.

My third career highlight came during the 1989 Super Bowl in Miami. A few months before, I was one of five NFL players selected to participate in the 1989 Diet Pepsi Super Bowl Talent Competition. The competition was hosted by Ahmad Rashaad and the late great John Candy, and broadcasted live prior to the start of the big game. Millions of Super Bowl fans saw the competition. I sang "The Greatest Love of All." I thought I *had* won the competition and so did my family and friends. However, it wasn't meant to be. But it didn't matter. My friends and family members who saw the competition told me that I was "robbed" and, at the end of the day, all I remember is that I sang at the SUPER BOWL!

My fourth career highlight could be called "Da Fellas!" Because my NFL career was cut short, I'm routinely asked by family and friends if I miss playing the game. My answer has always been "NO!" Why? Because football is a grueling sport. And football, if played on a high level, requires a nearly year-round commitment of an athlete's body, mind and heart. Put simply, football is hard! And the sacrifices required to play football are real. I and many of my colleagues have risked life and limb and sacrificed a considerable amount of time with family, friends and hobbies for the game. Consequently, many of us played football not so much because of a love for the game but rather for the rewards associated with it.

My Teammates

One reward that comes with playing football is being a part of a locker room. A typical college or NFL locker room is populated by guys with different backgrounds, different abilities, different life experiences, and from different parts of the United States. There are guys who look like they play football and guys who don't. There are married guys and single guys. Guys with children and guys without. Guys who are into politics and those who aren't. There are guys who see football as a means *to* an end and those who see football as *the* end. However, what makes the locker room so incredibly special and rewarding is not that it's composed of a diverse group of individuals, but rather, that each individual in this diverse group has decided to put aside all their differences to play football together as a team.

Not surprisingly, a common objective for every football team is to win football games. And everyone knows that to win games, a team must work together and play together. To that end, in a locker room, no one is overly concerned about how "different" a player might be. The overriding focus is on their contribution to the team's goal, winning games. A locker room gives a glimpse into how awesome life can be in a diverse society when individuals focus on the major and not major in the minor – a true brotherhood! This is why I and many other football players refer to our teammates as "brothers." From St. Anthony School to the Detroit Lions, I've been blessed to have several teammates that I routinely introduce to others as my brothers. A representative list of my "brothers" includes the following: from CHS – Eric Roquemore, Frankie Divittorio, Robert McDonald, Daryl May, Vince Leggio and Brian "Big Red" Wampold;[21] from LSU – James Britt, Alan Risher, Al Richardson, Hermon Fontenot, Junius Dural, Mike Breaux, Eugene Daniel, Gene Lang, Leonard Marshall, Verge Ausberry, Dalton Hillard, Jerry Blake, Chris Cruz, Garland Jean-Batiste, Clint Berry, Lance Smith Mike Gambrell and Mike Cobb; from USL – Quintin Thomas, R.C. Mullin, Patrick Taylor, Patrick Broussard, Tim Williams, Wade Butler, Rich Gannon, Thomas Jackson, Van Ray Alexander, Todd Scott, Brian Mitchell and Thomas King; and from the Lions – Scott Williams, George Jamison, James Jones, Tim Arnold, Eddie Murray, Carl Bland and Dewayne Galloway. These guys and several others – especially Tracy Lewis, my best friend since high school – brought a joy and a sense of accountability to my life that I cannot begin to describe and am just starting to truly appreciate. Guys like the above are the main reason why many of us who no longer play the game miss the game! And

---

[21] Big Red was special. Nobody worked harder or cared more about the guys in the locker room than Big Red. I don't have many regrets in life, but one I do have is not doing enough to nurture my friendship with Brian. I loved everything about Big Red, including his sister, Leslie, and her secret admirer and eventual husband Corey, whom I nicknamed "Cave-Man." Gone way too soon!!! When the "bell [finally] tolls for me," one of the first things I wanna do on the other side is get an arm-wrestling rematch with Big Red. When he beat me in high school, I wasn't ready! I wasn't! Seriously!

that's why I have no regrets regarding the length of time I played professionally. I'm just incredibly grateful that I got to play![22]

USL II

Danny Cottonham

---

[22] Although I'm no longer a part of a "locker room," I am a member of a prayer line called Men Praying Together, or MPT. Similar to a college or NFL locker room, MPT consist of a group of guys with various backgrounds, professions and life experiences. The members of MPT have two things in common: 1) we all believe in Jesus and the power of corporate prayer, and 2) we all love to fellowship. MPT was established in March 2003 and is still going strong today. The members of MPT call in on a conference line every weekday morning to pray together!

Like I mentioned above, my first academic semesters at USL were the worst in my life. But I didn't give in or give out. Instead, I got to know a man that every student athlete at USL called Mr. C. – Dean Danny Cottonham.

Mr. C. was the director of USL's Student Athlete Academic Center and Dean of Academics for all student athletes, male and female. Mr. C. loved his job, and he loved working with student athletes. He genuinely wanted every athlete at USL to graduate, on time. To that end, every semester, Mr. C. and his staff worked tirelessly assisting over 300 student athletes with class scheduling; this included selecting the "right" classes (to graduate on time), at the "right" time (not to interfere with team commitments) and with the "right" professors (who supported USL athletics). Additionally, Mr. C. implemented a "class check" procedure which would alert him and his staff if an athlete missed class. If an athlete was having problems with a particular course, Mr. C. and his staff did everything possible to ensure that every athlete got the help he or she needed, usually by providing access to tutors.

Life had gotten really complicated after I left Coach Stovall's office. I constantly wondered if I'd made the right decision, and my petroleum engineering classes were downright hard. Because Mr. C's class check procedure had a grade check component, he quickly found out that I was struggling academically. In the past, to overcome my academic woes, I would simply spend more time studying, and that usually fixed the problem. That's what I did in my second year at USL, 1985, and I was able to get myself off of academic probation. However, I still wasn't making the grades I was used to or the kinda grades I wanted to show my parents. 1984 and 1985 were without a doubt the toughest years of my young adult life. I wasn't doing well academically, nor was I doing well in football. For me, it was the "worst of times." Ironically, however, because of Mr. C, the "worst of times" were also the "best of times."

Friends Are Essential

From my first day on campus until I left to play for the Lions, Mr. C was the best friend a guy could ever hope or pray for. First, he was only about ten years older than I was, which meant most of the time he knew what I was feeling without me having to explain very much. Second, Mr. C was cool. He always saw the big picture. He constantly reminded me that if I kept trying, if I kept believing, everything would work out for my good. Third, you couldn't look at Mr. C and feel sorry for yourself for very long – Mr. C was paralyzed from the waist down. But if you closed your eyes and just listened to him speak, you would never know that he was dealing with unbelievable challenges on a daily basis. Mr. C was and is one of a kind.

Because Mr. C believed that my academic and athletic struggles would eventually end, he repeatedly told me that I needed some friends. Before long, he began introducing me to members of the Theta Nu Chapter of his fraternity, Kappa Alpha Psi, Inc. After meeting a few of his fraternity brothers and doing some of my own research about Kappa Alpha Psi, I called my dad to get his opinion about pledging, or joining a fraternity. To my surprise, my dad told me about several of our relatives who were longtime members of KAΨ. He even said he'd wanted to pledge Kappa when he was in college but couldn't because of his commitment to the GSU marching band and gigging (my dad played saxophone in a band that performed in venues all over Louisiana). Long story short, my dad told me to go ahead and pledge.

Because Mr. C understood what I and other student athletes were dealing with on and off the field, he and a few of his fraternity brothers, led by Dwayne Murray (who eventually became a two-term Grand Polemarch/President of Kappa Alpha Psi, Inc.), petitioned KAΨ's regional and national leadership for permission to do something that had never been done in the fraternity's storied history: have a summer pledge line. To everyone's surprise, KAΨ, Inc., approved a summer line in 1984. I and several other athletes expressed a strong interest in taking advantage of this opportunity. However, when the "Big Brothers" came knocking on the doors of all those who'd expressed an interest, I was the only one who answered the call. I pledged by myself: one unit, one part!

Ironically, once again, I had no one to talk to, no one to share with and no one to hang out with. My pledge period was tough. It was hard. It was grueling. To this day, I don't know how I made it! But I did. I thank God for my DP (Dean of Pledges), Stephone Addison, Rollo Cormier (who treated me like a brother before I became a "brother") and the chapter

Polemarch, the late Calvin Lain. Though I didn't have any friends when I pledged, once I crossed "the burning sands" I was able to form relationships and friendships that have lasted to this day. Mr. C was right. After I gained a few friends – or better yet, a few brothers – life, even with all its frustrations, was good again![23] But that's not all.

Get Help

Mr. C was well aware of the type of student I wanted to be. Hence, he introduced me to the idea of getting a tutor to assist me with my studies. Sounds simple enough. But for a guy who had never had a tutor and had always found a way to figure things out on his own, getting a tutor seemed like waving the white flag of surrender! Nevertheless, after I was forced to retire from the NFL, reality started to set in that I was going to need a job – a real job. Clearly, in order to be employed as a petroleum engineer, I had to improve my GPA. A former professional athlete graduating in engineering sounds good, but it was no guarantee that I would get hired. So I swallowed my pride, took Mr. C's advice and hired a tutor.

Hiring a tutor was one of the best decisions I've ever made in my academic life. My tutor was from China, but he spoke perfect English and could explain complex engineering concepts in a way that I could actually visualize what he was saying. Going to class finally became enjoyable again!

When I retired from football, I had three academic semesters left before graduation. Because I followed Mr. C's advice, they were my best semesters at USL. I not only completed the requirements to receive a Bachelor of Science in Petroleum Engineering, but prior to graduation, I was awarded a Chevron Engineering Scholarship, named the 1989-1990 American Petroleum Institute's Outstanding Senior in USL's Petroleum Engineering Department – and Marathon Oil Company extended an offer to me to work in its production engineering department in Lafayette, LA, which I accepted! I was also awarded USL's Buddy Marine Outstanding Student Athlete award, which is not awarded annually, only when a student

---

[23] In 1988, I was recognized by the Theta Nu Chapter of Kappa Alpha Psi for "Outstanding Achievement and Contributions."

athlete satisfies certain criteria. Needless to say, on graduation day, May 13, 1990, my parents were proud and I was very happy. Thanks Mr. C!

Work Fathers

Marathon Oil Company

Background

I accepted the job offer from Marathon Oil Company (MOC) before graduation, and started working one month after my graduation, in June 1990. MOC engages in the exploration and production of oil and gas. When I started, MOC's Lafayette office was responsible for the company's Gulf of Mexico/offshore operations. I was assigned to the production-workover department, which was responsible for enhancing the production of MOC's existing wells and for "completing" each oil and/or gas well once drilled to and through a designated location. Most if not all of the wells my department was responsible for were in the Gulf and were only accessible via helicopter or workboat.

Before working at MOC, I had never set foot on an oil rig, offshore or otherwise, and I had never flown in a helicopter or traveled on a workboat. Though I had a good understanding of what my job entailed, my understanding was all theoretical, which meant I was completely unprepared to do the job I was hired for! I had to learn how to perform my job duties and responsibilities while on the job, and I had to learn fast. My supervisor expected me to perform well completion and well workover projects, without supervision, in 12 months or less. Notably, the costs for many of the projects in my department were well over $3 million.

Randy Vincent

To say I was nervous and a little scared would be an understatement. I didn't know any of the engineers in my department; there weren't any from USL. Once again, I found myself by myself. Then lightning struck! A few days after I was hired, MOC hired another engineer, Randy Vincent. Prior to joining MOC, Randy had worked in the oil industry for several years and he was a USL graduate. Randy had also played football in high school. As soon as I was introduced to Randy, we became fast friends. We ate together. We drank together. We enjoyed the same type of music and we loved sports and making pretty girls smile. Most importantly, Randy was a very smart, down-to-earth, experienced workover/completions engineer. He could converse with the brainiacs in the department as well as with the roughnecks on the rigs. Everybody either loved Randy or was jealous of him. I loved him.

Because of our friendship, the department supervisor allowed me to accompany Randy on his offshore assignments. Randy was the senior engineer/teacher and I was the junior engineer/student. Knowing that I had never been offshore before, Randy immediately began teaching me about offshore life – starting with the dos and don'ts of helicopter flights and how to get on and off a workboat. He taught me the importance of estimating, monitoring, understanding and appreciating pressure. And he impressed upon me the importance of having a good working relationship with the drilling engineer and the rig hands. Because of the dangers associated with drilling and well completion work, he explained, it was imperative that I learned to trust the guys I worked with and that they learned to trust me. He said that the quickest way to build trust was to make sure my calculations were correct, i.e., no do-overs. Being around Randy reminded me of being with my dad.

Randy also made me keenly aware that aside from the cooks and cafeteria workers, I would probably be the only black person on the entire platform/rig, which housed about 75 men at any given time. He told me this to prepare me for the looks I would get and the conversations I would overhear. But Randy also reminded me to focus on one thing – my job. To do it and do it well. He told me that I had one major advantage that would insulate me from a lot problems with the rig hands – word was spreading to all MOC platforms in the Gulf that MOC had hired an engineer who'd played in the NFL. Randy was right. Because I'd played pro football, whenever I landed on a platform, no matter who I had to work with, I was treated like an old friend or a celebrity.

I took notes on everything Randy said and did for three solid months. While I was under his supervision, he let me take the reins on two of his assignments. I did well, and he reported my progress to our supervisors. As a result, I "broke out" on my own within six months of employment – a first at MOC. Eventually, I was placed in charge of the day-to-day production of more than 50 offshore oil and gas wells, which produced 6,000 barrels of oil and 15 million standard cubic feet of natural gas per day. With the help of my MOC colleagues, I developed and implemented completion and workover projects totaling well over $30 million and received a performance rating of "Excellent" for three consecutive years. I also reduced the estimated operating cost for one of my projects by $1 million within my first 12 months at MOC. Because Randy helped me, I do my best to help others! Thanks Randy!

Loyola School of Law

Background

You might remember from the first chapter that when I was a kid, I wanted to be a superhero when I grew up. But if I couldn't be a real superhero, I wanted to become a lawyer. This dream was cemented in my heart and mind after meeting Brace Godfrey, as discussed above, and because of my desire to help others – more on this below – but also because of my admiration for my late aunt, Joan Bernard Armstrong, former Chief Judge of the Louisiana Fourth Circuit Court of Appeal and *the* first female ever elected to the "bench" in Louisiana.[24] My aunt knew I wanted to become a lawyer, but she encouraged me to pursue *all* of my dreams: football, music/singing, engineering, etc. She would always say, "Baby, you can go to law school any time, now or later, so do it all."

And so, after working for MOC for three years and after arguably "doing it all," I got the law school bug! The bug was extremely potent. I started reading everything I could find about the law and law school,

---

[24] My Aunt, Judge Joan Bernard Armstrong, will be featured in the book entitled *Lessons from My Mothers*.

including novels about lawyers and law firms. Soon I was having a difficult time staying focused on my engineering job. I knew I had to resign my position; I had no choice. But before I left MOC, I applied for admission at Loyola School of Law in New Orleans, where a portrait of my aunt is still on display. When I was accepted and offered a scholarship to attend Loyola, I was overjoyed. I enrolled at Loyola School of Law in the fall of 1993.

Most of Loyola's professors employed the Socratic method when teaching their respective courses. Because I was an older student and because of everything I'd already been through, I was not very worried about the Socratic teaching method (which was a mistake). In fact, in the lead-up to my first semester, family and friends who heard about my seismic move from engineering to law school told me that law school would be a cinch for "someone like me." Unfortunately, I believed them. They repeatedly reminded me of my prior accomplishments: CHS Grizzly Great, former NFL player, 1989 Super Bowl contest participant, API's Outstanding Senior in Petroleum Engineering and Outstanding Student Athlete, and an MOC engineer. However, what they nor I realized was that law school was completely different from anything that I had ever experienced before. I went from a world where success and failure could be readily determined by objective, easily seen or ascertained factors and criteria to a world of "it depends." And I went from a world where everyone admired football players to a world where some of my colleagues sincerely questioned my desire to voluntarily participate in a "collision" sport and subject myself to potentially life-threatening injuries on a regular basis.

Nevertheless, when one of my law professors posed a probing question to the class, I would often make the mistake of raising my hand in an effort to get his or her attention and provide "the" answer. As you might imagine, I ate many slices of humble pie during my first 30 days as a 1L. However, there was a silver lining to the self-inflicted wounds I sustained. Some of my classmates admired my fearlessness and the manner in which I expressed my thoughts. As a result, I was invited to join several study groups.

I eventually joined a study group that consisted of two guys, Greg Mier and Keith Hall, and four ladies, Olga Bogran, Chandell Gautreaux, Karen Matherne and Valerie Sercovich. To say we learned a lot from each other and enjoyed our study sessions would be an understatement. We learned a lot because we were all very different and thus saw life's events, good and bad, from different perspectives. We enjoyed our study sessions because we were mature enough to be respectful of our differences. Rarely did anyone get offended if someone challenged his or her conclusions. For us, our study group was a way to ensure we were thinking and analyzing our course material correctly. Slowly but surely, we started analyzing law school hypothets with the relevant state or federal statutes and case law as opposed to relying on our "feelings" and personal thoughts. Though being a part of a good study group was essential to my success in law school, I personally needed more.

Michael DuBos

Who You Meet Can Change How You Think

During my first semester in law school, it became abundantly clear to me which classes I would do very well in and which classes would pose a problem. The more concrete the analysis, the easier the class. The more abstract the analysis, well… Because success in all my classes was essential to gaining employment post law school, I knew I needed help (thanks Mr. C.). Unbeknownst to me, help was on the way. Around the beginning of my second semester, I was introduced to a guy named Michael DuBos, or "Mickey." I don't remember how we met, but I'm sure glad we did.

When we met, Mickey was a 2L and I was a 1L. We were both married and loved sports. I was relatively tall, dark, muscular and handsome, and Mickey was not! (LOL) But Mickey had a seemingly photographic memory and I did not. Additionally, Mickey was fast and I was not. He talked fast, worked fast and wrote fast. Equally as impressive, Mickey had a sense of humor that rivaled any standup comic. Mickey and I became fast friends. Though it was clear why I befriended Mickey, at first I didn't really know why he befriended me. As it turned out, we not only liked each other, we needed each other.

After just a few conversations with Mickey, it was abundantly clear that he had a God-given gift for making the most abstract concepts more concrete and the most complex law school fact pattern plain. I started hanging around Mickey every chance I got. I played golf with Mickey. I ate lunch and dinner with Mickey. I drank with Mickey. I even shared my life experiences with Mickey. Incredibly, just by being around him, I learned how to more effectively outline a law school class and how to better reduce a fact pattern to its material elements. My ability to quickly express my thoughts in essay form increased dramatically. Before long, I was kinda enjoying law school! In fact, I was even asked to join a few organizations and was voted President of the Black Law Students Association. Though my opportunity to make law review, for all intents and purposes, ended after I made two mediocre grades in my first semester, by the time I entered my final year of law school, I had employment offers from some of the most prestigious law firms in Louisiana and Mississippi, some of which I'd never even clerked for. Though many attribute my employment opportunities to my prior life experiences, I know the truth, and now you do too![25]

---

[25] Mickey and I have remained friends since law school. Because his home is located in north Louisiana, after law school, I spent a considerable amount of time in that area. At least twice a year, our families camped out together. While camping, I was in charge of cooking and telling stories to the kids around the campfire. Mickey took care of just about everything else: preparing the campsite, constructing a zipline and making sure

Because I enjoyed my job as a petroleum engineer, when I left MOC to attend law school, instead of resigning, I took a two-year educational leave of absence. I had every intention of returning to MOC as a member of their legal team in Houston. However, while I was being taught how to think like a lawyer, I was also yearning for a deeper, more abiding relationship with God through Jesus Christ. Because of my relationship with a few good men, after graduating from law school and passing the Louisiana State Bar Exam, I decided not to return to MOC. Instead, I accepted an associate's position at a law firm in New Orleans.

When I was a young boy, Pastor Charles T. Smith and the Shiloh Missionary Baptist Church family, along with my parents, established a belief system within me on which I still stand today. I believe in one God who exists in three equally divine persons: the Father, the Son and the Holy Spirit. I believe that God is actively involved in creation and provides needed counseling, direction and correction in the person of the Holy Spirit, the Bible, people and circumstances. And I believe that Jesus Christ is God the Son, whose death, burial and resurrection made it possible for me to become part of the family of God. Nevertheless, because of my "humanity," applying what I believe to life's many and varied dilemmas has always been challenging. Thankfully, I was introduced to three men who have helped me navigate life's twists and turns.

---

we had enough canoes and four-wheelers. Because of our friendship, I've become friends with Mickey's friends and his pastor, Greg Clark, Senior Pastor at Cedar Crest Baptist Church. Eventually, I even became an honorary member of the Cedar Crest Mass Choir and was their featured soloist on numerous occasions.

Spiritual Fathers

Pastor Lloyd Joiner, Jr.

Pastor Lloyd Joiner, Jr. is the Senior Pastor at Progressive Baptist Church in Lafayette, Louisiana. Though I attended Progressive while at USL, I really didn't get to know Pastor Joiner until after I graduated and went to work for MOC. By all accounts, Pastor Joiner has been and continues to be an outstanding pastor. However, that is not why he's included in this book. I'm writing about Pastor Joiner because of who he is, not because of what he does. Specifically, he was the first pastor that I've ever been able to truly call my friend. His infectious smile drew me to his ministry as a college student, but his heart convinced me that love can change a life.

I've observed Pastor Joiner in his role as Progressive's Senior Pastor, where on Sunday mornings and midweek services he routinely gives hope to all in attendance and, after the benediction, effortlessly deescalates concerns, disputes and dilemmas without causing anyone to feel small or insignificant. I've also played golf with Pastor Joiner and his friends. Everyone who plays golf knows that a bad golf shot can tempt the most devout Christian to "lay his or her religion down" in a sand bunker and leave it there. But not Pastor Joiner. Unlike anyone else I've ever golfed with, Pastor Joiner quotes scripture to describe just about all his golf shots, good or bad. And he does it not to preach, but to remind everyone to have fun. If he drives his golf ball off the tee box 200+ yards and it lands in the fairway, you may hear him say, "Looks like I found the Roman Road to Salvation." If he almost makes a difficult putt, he might say "That's what King Agrippa told the Apostle Paul – thou almost persuadest me to be a Christian."

To my surprise, by just hanging around Pastor Joiner outside of church, I began to understand how to remain true to my faith without sounding like a wannabe pastor or minister, or someone who doesn't think they need the grace and mercy of God on a daily basis. I even learned how to do a better job of seeing the best in people and in myself. Hanging around Pastor Joiner truly convinced me that "everything [in my life] is going to be alright." Everything! Equally as important, being with Pastor Joiner reminded me that the God who made the heavens and the earth isn't just concerned about women and children, he's also concerned about and in love with men, including me! That friendly reminder set my "mind" free. Unfortunately, for a time, I really believed that God was primarily or only concerned about women and children and not really concerned about men or me. Thus, nearly every time I prayed and asked the Father for something/anything I would always end my prayer by saying how that "something/anything" would or could benefit others, especially women and children. Because I believed that God wasn't really "that" concerned about me, I had to be concerned about me. Thus, for a period of time, nearly all my thoughts/dreams, when I wasn't praying, were centered on me: my desires, my needs and my goals. Being reminded that God is actually concerned about and in love with me as a man changed my thought life.

Now, because I truly believe that God is thinking about me and is concerned about me, sometimes when I pray, I petition the Father for myself and only me, without adding any tag lines about others. Additionally, because I know that God is concerned about my needs and my goals, I don't worry about my personal welfare as much. Now, I think a lot about the welfare of others. Consequently, after I retired from the NFL, I became a "real" volunteer.[26]

For instance, one Sunday morning, Pastor Joiner expressed a need for the men of the church to play a more active role in the lives of the young boys in the community. In response, with the help of Deacon Leo Bolden, I formed an organization called Operation Kids. Our mission was to show several disadvantaged young boys the love of God by giving them an opportunity to be children. A good friend told me about a housing project called Holy Family where many young boys lived with only one parent, mainly their mothers. One afternoon I traveled to Holy Family and met with a few mothers and said that I'd like to take their sons on a field trip every Saturday afternoon and Sunday morning. Not surprisingly, having played in the NFL and being employed at MOC gave me instant credibility, and the moms readily agreed to let their sons be part of Operation Kids. They signed the necessary liability waivers and committed to getting the boys dressed and ready to go on time.

Just about every Saturday for nearly two years, Leo and I would pick up seven to ten young boys from Holy Family and allow them the freedom to act their age, i.e., to do whatever they wanted to do. It didn't matter. If they wanted to see a movie, we'd take them to a theater. If they wanted to go to an all-you-can-eat buffet, that's where we ate. If they wanted to drive go-carts, attend a Saints home game, a ULL football or basketball game, go on a camping trip or to an arcade, or go bowling… we did it. Their wish was truly our command. The only condition we placed on the boys was that they had to accompany Leo and me to Sunday school at Progressive on Sunday mornings (except if we were going to a Saints game). We had nearly 100% participation. Operation Kids eventually expanded into an after-school tutoring program which provided assistance in math, English and reading comprehension. Needless to say, the boys and their moms were very appreciative of our efforts, and Pastor Joiner was overjoyed. In fact,

---

[26] In fact, a Kiwanis Club in Lafayette, LA, in recognition of my contributions to the Lafayette community, honored me with a Key to the City of Lafayette. Additionally, I became a volunteer at the Veterans Administration Hospital in New Orleans and

when I had an opportunity to visit Progressive some 20 years later, Pastor Joiner informed me that the tutoring program was still going strong.[27] I was blown away!

On another Sunday morning, Pastor Joiner declared that it was time to build a larger edifice to accommodate the growing congregation. He then challenged certain members of the congregation to see who could raise the most money for the church's building fund. The winner would receive an all-expenses-paid week-long trip to Jamaica. When Pastor Joiner made the announcement, because my thought life had changed, I didn't ignore his plea; I took on the challenge and eventually discovered that Jamaica is a great place to vacation!!! I won by a margin of nearly $50,000. The new edifice was and continues to be a landmark for the people in the community and evidence of what God can do when his people are focused not only on their own needs but also on the needs of others.

My relationship with Pastor Joiner changed my life. It's thanks to him that I became a doer, not just for myself and my family, but for my community. So much so that when I see a problem, instead of asking God to do something, I ask him to help me to do something. Thanks Pastor Joiner.

---

organized a group of twenty men to travel to Moore, Oklahoma and Tuscaloosa, Alabama to assist local residents with post-tornado clean-up of buildings and debris.
[27] Every now and then when I'm in the Lafayette area, I run into a few of the "boys." Even though many of them have families of their own, they never let me forget about the investment we made in them some thirty plus years ago.

Bishop Paul S. Morton

When I first moved to New Orleans to attend law school, I would travel to Lafayette just about every weekend to attend Sunday morning services at Progressive. However, once I realized how much time I needed to succeed in my first-semester courses, my weekend traveling came to an abrupt end. As a result, I began looking for a church to attend and possibly join in New Orleans. I asked several of my Baptist colleagues who were from New Orleans for a recommendation. A few suggested Greater St. Stephen (GSS) – a nontraditional Baptist "megachurch" with 20,000 members and growing fast – but the majority of my colleagues suggested a different church.

One Sunday morning, my wife and I were getting ready to attend the church that most of my colleagues had suggested, but she was taking an extra-long time getting dressed. That church's worship service began at 11:00 am, but it was clear we wouldn't make it on time. Knowing that I didn't like being late for anything, she suggested that we go to GSS that Sunday. GSS had two locations in New Orleans, an Uptown campus and an East campus, and multiple Sunday services were held at each location. There was a 12:30 service at GSS' Uptown location, so we decided to attend that service.

We arrived about 20 minutes early, and the church was already packed. The service started a few minutes early with a call to worship, followed by praise and worship. I had never experienced praise and worship like I experienced that day. Everybody on the praise team could sing, and I mean really *sing*. Every musician could play, and I mean really *play*. And most if not all of the songs were songs *to* God, not just *about* God. When I caught on to the songs, for one of the few times in my life, I felt as though I was at God's holy altar singing to *him*, not singing to *people* about him. I was blown away. I felt an intimacy with God that I'd never experienced before in my life. Praise and worship lasted approximately 15 minutes, during which time I cried, I repented, I was forgiven and I was strengthened. I looked at my wife and asked if she'd been super late on purpose. She nodded. She later told me that many of our friends at Progressive had suggested we attend GSS, but she didn't tell me because GSS was "nontraditional." She knew that, at this time in my life, the only way I would go to a nontraditional church was if it was too late to attend the other recommended church on time. She was right.

After the offering service, GSS' Senior Pastor, Bishop Paul S. Morton, led a worship song to prepare the congregation to receive the "preached word."[28] His hymn of preparation was also a song sung to God and not to the church. Man, could he sing, and I mean really sing. When he finished the hymn, the level of expectation and anticipation to hear the word was so thick that it could be cut with a knife and so high that it felt like at any moment members of the congregation would break out running. When Bishop Morton began preaching, he didn't "declare" or "proclaim" the word from the pulpit as I expected, nor did he sound preachy. Instead,

---

[28] Bishop Morton became the Senior Pastor of Greater Saint Stephen in 1975. Following his appointment, GSS grew from 647 members to over 20,000 while expanding from one location to three in the New Orleans metro area, offering eight weekly worship services: five on Sunday, two midweek Bible studies and a Friday night Deliverance Service. In 1992, Bishop Morton, with the assistance of senior pastors from across the country, founded and established the Full Gospel Baptist Church Fellowship International.

he took the congregation on a journey, a journey about the life and times of Jesus Christ. In other words, he told a story about Jesus. The story was told from the perspective of one of the disciples but with a technique that made it relevant for the 21st-century listener.

Bishop Morton's demeanor at this time could be described as joyous and loving. You could literally see the joy in his heart and feel the love he had for Jesus and the congregation, which immediately let me know that he, himself, was fully persuaded that Jesus was and is the answer. At the conclusion of his sermon, I and everyone around me were clearly convinced and/or convicted. I was so moved, I wanted to accept Jesus Christ as my personal savior all over again! The service was breathtaking. And, when compared to a more traditional Baptist church, the service was short! That service was over in just an hour and 15 minutes; we were walking out of the church around 1:45pm. GSS was truly a nontraditional Baptist church. LOL! I even thanked my wife for being late!! Not many months later, we became members of GSS.

Becoming a member at GSS and having Bishop Morton as my pastor took me to a new level of intimacy with God and allowed me to better define the purpose for my life. Like I said, GSS was considered a nontraditional Baptist church. One reason is because the church's leadership placed great emphasis on the purpose and functionality of the Holy Spirit within the life of the believer. As a result, every service was a reminder that God is not only *with* us but also *in* us in the person of the Holy Spirit. When I began to embrace this concept on a practical level, I realized that I truly have the power to change my life and my world. The key was to learn to trust and obey the promptings within me that line up with the written word of God and/or his profound love for people. This tenet or principle caused me to spend more time learning about God through the person of Jesus Christ. As a result, now, I strive to love others as I believe Jesus loves me. Eventually, I became a deacon/servant leader on the GSS Deacon Board and, not long thereafter, became the Board's Chairman.

As discussed above, I joined GSS while in law school. As a student, I was clear about two things. First, I knew I wanted to be a lawyer. And second, I had a pretty good idea of the areas of law that I wanted to practice in. However, I had no clue how I wanted to present myself and my client's case, nor the style of communication I would use before a judge or a jury.

That is, until I was introduced to Bishop Morton's style of advocacy. After witnessing the effectiveness of presenting a case in the form of a story and in an atmosphere of joy and love, I knew I had discovered my advocacy style. My decision was solidified after witnessing hundreds of individuals, week after week, flock to the altar to accept Christ as their personal savior at the conclusion of Bishop Morton's "closing argument."

From that point on, every opportunity I received to speak before a group, I presented the subject in the form of a story with a joyous and loving demeanor. I even utilized this advocacy style during a two-week trial skills advocacy training session hosted by the National Institute for Trial Advocacy (NITA) at its National Session in Louisville, CO. Over 100 young lawyers from around the world were in attendance. At the conclusion of the program, the program director informed me that the program instructors all agreed that I was one of the top two lawyers at the session and that they wanted me to consider becoming a NITA Trial Advocacy Instructor. I accepted the challenge and eventually enrolled in NITA's Advocacy Teacher Training Program in San Francisco, CA. After completing the professional teacher training skills program, I became a certified NITA Trial Ad Instructor and later became a Trial Ad Instructor at LSU's Paul M. Hebert Law Center. Employing the above-mentioned style of advocacy has helped me win many trials and resolve numerous cases in both federal and state courts across the Gulf-South. Thanks Bishop!

At an NFL Former Players Conference held in New Orleans, a conference speaker asked the guys in attendance this question: At what time in your life were you the most productive? Though I and the other players gave a variety of answers, there was one common denominator: during the most productive periods of our lives, we all had a coach encouraging us to give our best and be our best. After much discussion, the takeaway from that meeting was the following: to be productive in any particular area of your life, you need a coach!

Fortunately for me, Dr. Benny Jones, who, at the time, was the president of the Fellowship of Christian Athletes' Louisiana Chapter, invited me to be the featured singer at an FCA Prayer Luncheon at the Louisiana High School Athletic Association's Coaches Clinic.[29] After my performance, Dr. Jones introduced me to Coach Jerry Baldwin, who, at the time, was an assistant football coach at LSU and the Huddle leader for LSU's FCA chapter.[30] Coach Baldwin invited me to speak at an LSU FCA midweek chapter meeting that began at 7:00pm. When I arrived, there were nearly 150 LSU student athletes in attendance – by far the largest FCA Huddle I'd ever attended. I was blown away! That night I decided that I had to get to know Coach Baldwin. I had to get to know the man who could motivate that many college athletes to attend a midweek religious service at night!

Worth noting, when I met Coach Baldwin, I was a first-year associate attorney at a mid-major oil and gas law firm in New Orleans. At that time, I and another associate attorney were given the freedom and responsibility to develop a sports law practice at the firm. Because of my background in football, I focused most of my time and energy on athlete and athletic coach representation. Thus, to get to know Coach Baldwin, I convinced him to hire me as his agent.

As Coach Baldwin's agent, my primary responsibility was to secure him a head coaching job at a Division 1-A university. In the process of working for him, I got to know a man unlike anyone I had ever met. I observed him at home enjoying time with his wife and two daughters, and I observed him on the football field positioning young boys to become future millionaires while demonstrating to his coaching colleagues that

---

[29] As mentioned above, I became a member of FCA while at CHS. Not long after I began practicing law, I was asked to become a member of FCA's Board of Directors for its Louisiana Chapter and assisted the president of FCA's Louisiana Chapter, Dr. Benny Jones, as directed. Because of my affiliation with FCA, for nearly 15 years I was a featured soloist at the Allstate Sugar Bowl Prayer Breakfast and a pre-game chapel speaker for numerous NFL and university football teams.

[30] Prior to joining the coaching staff at LSU, Coach Baldwin had received five Coach of the Year honors in eight years as a high school football coach. Later on, he became the first African American to be named Assistant Head Football Coach at Louisiana Tech (1983-1993) and at LSU (1993-1995) and was also the top recruiter of high school talent at both colleges. Moreover, while transforming young boys into productive men, Coach Baldwin was and still is the Senior Pastor at New Living Word Ministries in Ruston, Louisiana.

adhering to biblical principles and winning in life and in football can go hand in hand. I've watched him motivate hundreds of people to love one another from his pulpit at New Living Word Ministries and at various conference and banquet podiums across Louisiana. I've spent many evenings observing how he uncannily unravels complex life dilemmas for his family and for others. I was there when he started an alternative school with his own money to educate at-risk youth after they were expelled from various Lincoln Parish public schools. Coach Baldwin provided these kids with an opportunity to continue their education. I've even ridden with him around Lincoln Parish, watching him gather homeless men and women off the streets and provide them *all* with housing, food, clothing and jobs. In fact, Coach Baldwin established seven restoration facilities for the homeless and the formerly incarcerated to give them a second chance at a productive life. Again, in my entire life I had never met another human being quite like Coach Jerry Baldwin, accomplishing feat after feat and overcoming obstacle after obstacle as if he were a superhero in human flesh.

On one fateful day, I found out the secret to Coach Baldwin's power. He told me it was derived from a woman who preached a one-sentence sermon. I asked who the woman was and what sentence she preached. To my surprise, Coach Baldwin told me that the woman was Mother Mary from the Bible and the one-sentence sermon she preached was:

WHATSOEVER HE SAITH UNTO YOU, DO IT!

Coach B taught me that no matter the problem, no matter the concern, no matter the crisis or dilemma, the answer is found in that one-sentence sermon. Needless to say, watching Coach Baldwin live out this sermon crystalized and synergized all the lessons I had learned from my fathers. Of course, on occasion I have trouble deciphering "[what] he saith unto [me]." When that happens, I call on my father, Coach/Pastor Jerry Baldwin.

For instance, early in my career as a business owner, I was spending as much money as I was earning – I was barely breaking even, at best, and it felt like I was always at the office. Because I was unable to decipher what "He" was saying to me, I asked Coach Baldwin for help. After explaining to him my dilemma, Coach Baldwin told me that I needed to adjust my business model. Specifically, he described my problem as "wanting to go big instead of grow big!" He was right. I wanted to *look good* before I *became good.* I cared about what others thought about me as much as I cared about what God thought about me! Coach Baldwin's advice has exponentially reduced the self-inflicted stress in my life. Now I attempt to maintain a mustard seed or "grow big" mindset in everything I do. And finally, I will never forget the time when I was trying to get God, through Christ Jesus, to perform a miracle in my life in the same manner that Jesus performed miracles in the bible days.

Several years ago, I was diagnosed with having myopia or nearsightedness and I wanted God to miraculously correct my vision. After praying for several weeks and after nearly getting into a car accident while driving home at night, I called Coach B and asked him what should I do or say to get God to correct my vision. In response, Coach B asked if had I visited a doctor. I told him yes. He then asked me what did the doctor say. I said the doctor indicated that I needed to wear prescription eyeglasses. Coach B asked if I had gotten the prescribed eyeglasses. I told him yes. He asked me to put the glasses on. I did. Then he asked me if I could see clearly with them on. I said yes. Coach B said "my boy I think you've been healed." We both started laughing! Then in Coach B fashion, he admonished me not to look for miracles when simply following instructions can solve the problem. Needless to say, that experience changed the way I look at life and my relationship with God. Thanks Coach B!

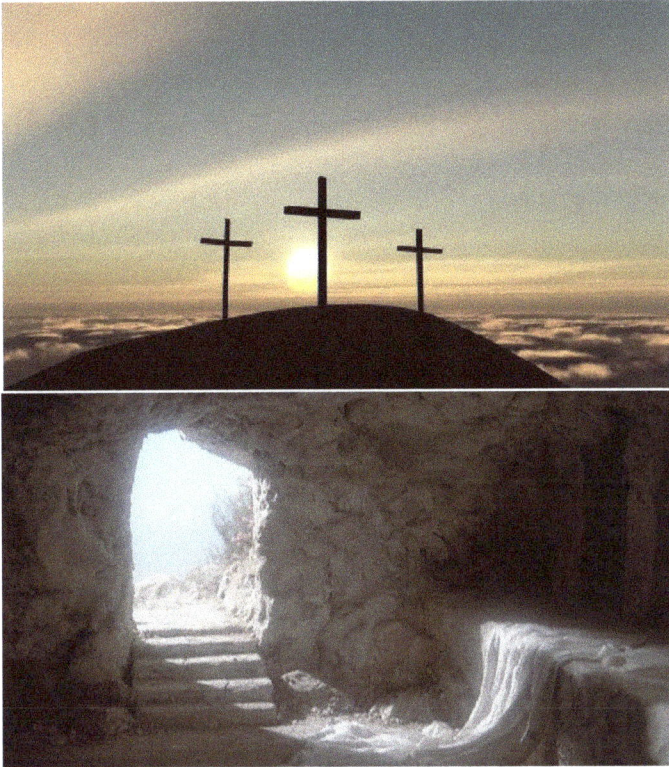

Finally, I'll end this book the way I began: by thanking God the Father for all of the "fathers" he's brought into my life to position me to become who I was born to be! Though I've accomplished many goals during my lifetime, I've also gone through situations that I would not wish on an enemy. Nevertheless, as I complete the third quarter of my life, I still wake up nearly every morning full of gratitude and with an expectation that something good is going to happen to me and around me. Now might be a good time to describe how I've been able to handle the successes and overcome the challenges in my life. I will in my next book entitled *The Ultimate Test: Who Do You Love the Most?* Stay tuned!

www.ingramcontent.com/pod-product-compliance
Lightning Source LLC
Chambersburg PA
CBHW041922090426
42741CB00019B/3449